WORCESTER
IN A DAY
SATURDAY 3 AUGUST 1968
IN OLD PHOTOGRAPHS

WORCESTER
IN A DAY
SATURDAY 3 AUGUST 1968
IN OLD PHOTOGRAPHS

MICHAEL DOWTY

ALAN SUTTON
1988

Alan Sutton Publishing Limited
Brunswick Road · Gloucester

First published 1988

British Library Cataloguing in Publication Data

Dowty, Michael
Worcester in a day : Saturday 3 August
1968 in old photographs.
1. Hereford and Worcester. Worcester,
1960–1969
I. Title
942.4'4856

ISBN 0-86299-482-9

Typesetting and origination by
Alan Sutton Publishing Limited.
Printed in Great Britain

INTRODUCTION

Like it or not, change is permanent. Every day it comes our way, packed in assorted shapes and sizes, according to the whims of others, or our own needs, ambitions, desires and imaginings, vain or otherwise. It may parade anonymously under assumed names like evolution, progress, modernisation and the way forward, but we needn't for a moment be fooled – it's all change, and it's here to stay.

Most of us accept some small measure of gentle change with fortitude, even eagerness when it happens to be of our own choice and making. What we deplore is the sweeping variety which overnight destroys long-loved areas and replaces them with blocks of characterless concrete. It was precisely this kind of sanctioned vandalism that caused Worcester to suffer a nasty attack of national notoriety in 1964, when Geoffrey Moorhouse opened 'The Sack of Worcester' to a wider audience in *The Guardian*, although the city was hardly alone in matters of desecration. Few places escaped the frequently indelicate touch of planners and developers, some of whom took a very long time to re-discover the virtues of brick.

This book concerns the 'post-sack' Worcester of 20 years ago, or, to be precise, a single day in its life, for the photographs were all taken between 6.15 a.m. and 9 p.m. on 3 August 1968. Meteorologically, it was a fairly typical summer Saturday, ranging from overcast to murky, with a promise of rain briefly fulfilled in the early afternoon, and a solitary flash of mid-morning sunlight to illuminate no more than one of the 340 views produced. The plan was simple: keep moving and record as many aspects of the day as possible. The entire collection was exhibited at the City Art Gallery, three weeks later, under the title: 'The City – From Dawn to Dusk in 3.4 Seconds', taking the average exposure time to have been a 1/100th of a second.

The camera's unique ability to freeze infinitesimal crumbs of life and serve them years later as tangible reminders of long-vanished and often forgotten realities, makes it something of a lazy man's notebook. If one picture is genuinely worth a thousand words, then here are a couple of hundred thousand or more, telling a simple story of city folk at a time when they had double-decker buses, three cinemas, old-fashioned traffic jams instead of gyratory ones, an electricity works and proper money. Girls in mini-skirts displayed long acres of their lower extremities and motor cyclists exposed uncrowned heads to the elements. There were no bus lanes, and the craze for pedestrian zones hadn't yet hit town. Those were the days – or should it in this case be 'that was the day'?

Twenty years on, the pictures – virtually all of them – have changed: Citibus reigns, there is one cinema split into three, the jams are differently the same, the last volts danced from the electricity works long ago, and we have become blessed by the greatest of all inflationary devices – decimalisation. The mini-skirt lives on, though no longer in the ascendant, whilst the compulsory crash-helmet cocoons the noisy rider from the sound of his own decibels. Bus lanes provide convenient escape routes when other ways are blocked (and sometimes when they are not) and pedestrianisation has become the rage of the age.

Those few examples are mere trivialities, compared to the overall catalogue of change to have hit the city in recent years. Though retaining basic shape and structure, it differs vastly in detail from the Worcester of 1968. The majority of its shops have changed address, had facelifts, suffered the indignity of takeover or gone out of business altogether. Traffic signs have been updated and re-sited to cater for altered ways and conditions. A Silver Street has been lost, a City Walls Road gained. A couple of churches have disappeared and the long-suffering telephone kiosk finds itself gradually replaced by a creation of minimal appeal and comfort. A transformed Corn Exchange now houses Habitat, whilst Angel Street's Fruit and Vegetable Market has forsaken Saturday stalls for sheltered shops.

In common with anywhere else on earth, Worcester is unlikely ever to become wholly right or wrong – the continually active natural and human forces of destruction and creation will see to that. But whatever its shortcomings, there is undeniable charm about a place which once straightened its landmark steeple prior to bulldozing the supporting church and rocking the tower's foundations, or dug-up a main street only hours before the car bearing the Royal visitor was scheduled to pass. Administrative blots of this order are a tiny price to pay for association with a city offering a wide variety of delights to visitor and resident alike, and which – should they tire of its attractions – at least has the decency to allow them relatively easy escape into some of the loveliest landscape to be found anywhere.

Format's confines have made pruning prudent. The 213 photographs selected are those thought most likely to have general appeal and interest. They appear in chronological order, together with original sequence numbers, and are captioned (apart from bracketed references to subsequent happenings) in the present tense, in an attempt to keep things flowing reasonably smoothly. However long or short your acquaintance with the city, there should be something to wring a tear, raise an eyebrow, wrest a wry smile or induce a hollow laugh. If, by any chance, you were born in Worcester in 1968 (especially on 3 August), arrived by alternative means, got married, or embarked on any other memorable venture — Happy Anniversary! Otherwise, the appropriate greeting would seem to be: have a nice day!

MICHAEL DOWTY

(1) WORCESTER BRIDGE, 6.15 a.m. strangely deserted and conserving its strength for the later onslaught. (Twenty years on, the foreground carriageway stands divided by additions calculated to ease a continuing problem. Yet still one thinks kindly of the wit whose 'Car-Strangled Spanner' appellation springs readily to mind.)

(2) ONE OF A KIND. The companion lamp, having offended the forces of mindlessness by its very presence, has been temporarily removed for remedial treatment.

(4) THE GLOVER'S NEEDLE in competition with other aspiring objects.

(5) ANGEL PLACE, 6.28 a.m. Too soon for buses or queues. The only life present is a man invisibly calling from the left-hand telephone kiosk.

(6) ANGEL STREET. In less than an hour, market traders will be arriving to set up stalls, next to the Horn & Trumpet. The parked van belongs to the Musicassette Supply Company.

(8) HIGH STREET, at its nort-west end, showing Johnson's, dry cleaners; Paige Gowns Ltd.;
James Lucking & Co. Ltd., opticians; Civic, radio dealers; Hutton, ladies' outfitters –
apparently empty; Oliver's, shoe retailers; Boot's, the chemists and Bobby & Co. Ltd.,
drapers and outfitters.

(10) HIGH STREET, at 6.35 a.m. according to the old Market Hall clock, speaking uncomfortably from its new support building, opposite the Guildhall. The less visible trading names are Slendos, Freeman Hardy & Willis, The Golden Lion, Turner's and — beneath the clock — Stanley Martin.

(11) PUMP STREET. The old Methodist Church closed in June 1965. On the right, its replacement surmounts a row of new shops and one of the entrances to Lichgate Shopping Precinct. The other slice of modernity – left of centre – awaits new occupants, having, in its old body, been known as 'Shapland's Corner'.

(13) HIGH STREET is having an early morning 'wash and brush-up' from a cleansing vehicle. In this view from the corner of Pump Street, Jerimain Ltd., ladies' outfitters, and Singer Sewing Machines Ltd., are neighbours to the city's oldest church, St Helen's, dating back to AD 680, but employed now as the County Records Office.

(17) THE SHAMBLES. Barely awake at this hour of the day. On the left-hand corner is Busby's, and on the other side of the street the nearest name is Maggs Ltd., gentlemen's outfitters.

(19) A VIEW OF PROGRESS, from Union Street. Erect a monstrous slab, plonk a couple of outsize lumps of Lego on top, and *voila*! you've enhanced the neighbourhood.

(20) MOTORISTS' HELTER-SKELTER. Another happy blend of old and new, and watch it at peak times, cheerfully spewing its contents, slap into the Friar Street jam.

(21) 44 FRIAR STREET. Listed in the Worcester Directory as: 'boot and shoe retailer', Henry Starkey keeps his shop's face firmly fixed in the past.

(22) SIDBURY, continuing up into College Street. The porta-cabin on the right is occupied by Street's, the printers. (Today, the same spot marks the southern end of City Walls Road.)

(23) FOR SALE – large, blank wall and open space. Suit Firing-Squad. What offers? On the other side of the wall are W. J. Bladder & Sons, motor-cycle dealers. (St Peter's Church was demolished about eight years later.)

(24) SIDBURY, from Edgar Street. (Today, Bygones – extreme left – is a corner shop, without having moved, thanks to City Walls Road.)

(25) STAFF PROBLEM? Martin's Bank, at the corner of High Street and Church Street.

(26) THE DAILY NEWS – folded, wrapped and deposited outside Universal Stationers in High Street. Question: how does it survive on a wet morning?

(29) LIFE OUTSIDE LITTLEWOOD'S, shortly after 7 a.m. and there is movement. Will the elevated, listing ladders soon be leaning against listed elevations?

(30) TRANSPORT TIME. Workers awaiting their coach in Deansway. A chunk of Technical College shares the background with the base of St Andrew's tower.

(33) SHABBILY SOMNOLENT SCHOOL OF DRINKING. The Duke of Wellington in Deansway. (The Elgar School of Music has since taken over and wiped the beer rings from the Bar piano – if there ever was one.)

(34) BROAD STREET, at 7.14 a.m., the time provided by Halford's clock. Other familiar names present include District Bank Ltd., H.H. Burrow, corsetière; R.S. Skan & Sons Ltd., tobacconists & gentlemen's hairdressers; Oliver's, shoe retailers; Midland Bank; the Crown Hotel. In the distance the International Stores stands on The Cross.

(36) ANGEL PLACE. Driver and conductor of a W4 Malvern Road bus are on board, patiently waiting for passengers at 7.25 a.m. – and isn't the bus shelter pretty? (Not any more it isn't, nor are the others that go with it.)

(37) CREATING A MARKET. The traders have arrived for the weekly putting-up of poles and laying-out of produce.

(38) MARKETING A CREATION. Lofting his gaze above Harrison and Dolittle, the pushmi-pullyu simultaneously studies Angel Street and Angel Place.

(39) A BIT OF A CLUTTER. The approach to Foregate Street Station, with a tobacconist's kiosk – formerly Skan's, a milk-vending machine and an arms aloft poster girl, triumphantly proclaiming: 'M.E.B. Invents Elastic Money'. (The scene has changed in twenty years – a canopy now keeps the rain at bay, and underneath the arch is a place to dream your dreams of getting away.)

(40) SHRUB HILL ROAD. Since the early part of the century, Heenan & Froude Ltd., have occupied this imposing building which had earlier associations with railway engineering and the Worcester Exhibition of 1882.

(41) HOLY TRINITY CHURCH. Sandwiched between two portions of Heenan's, it is destined for demolition, with its rotund Ronkswood replacement having been consecrated on 12 November 1965. (The site has become a car-park, serving those working in the area or playing at Worcester Snooker Centre.)

(43) LOWESMOOR, from in front of the Salvation Army Hall – (better known today as the Vesta Tilley Centre, an excellent – if seemingly incongruous – transition. See for yourself, if you haven't already done so.)

(44) LOWESMOOR AGAIN. A member of the daily cart – or barrow – company executes a nifty step, during an immaculate street routine.

(45 & 47) AND AGAIN AND AGAIN. Two further views of Lowesmoor. (Award yourself the CDM for spotting changes to have occurred in the first. There are no medals for crossing off the Harrington Hotel, the distant row of shops and Barker's Garage in the second.)

(50) ONCE UPON A TIME — there was all this space and nothing much to do with it. And an awful lot of it shows in a gloomy view from Railway Walk. (The late Selwyn Pearce-Higgins was a local rail enthusiast who dreamed of Worcester becoming the location for the National Rail Museum. What a shame the Yorkists won.)

(51) NEWSBOY. Slotting another one in from the bulging sack at Terrace Walk.

(52) RAIL TRAVEL. Alternative version on the lower slope of Terrace Walk.

(53) POSTERS. What the well-dressed hoarding is wearing on Rainbow Hill.

(56 & 57) ELGAR'S LAST HOME. 'Marl Bank', Rainbow Hill. How sad to see it so run-down and neglected. (Not to worry. It was demolished late the following year.)

(61) PARK'S BATHS. At least one swimmer has terminated an unpromising aquatic career here. Another – nameless, for reasons governed by an impeccable sense of diplomacy – was once concussed by the clothes-prop. (The baths were demolished in 1972.)

(63) FOREGATE STREET. The time has moved on to 8.30 a.m. and the city is getting busy. The bus from Ombersley Road carries advertising for Colmore Depot and H.A. Saunders Ltd., (remember Silver Wings Taxis?). The poster on the bridge is for W & F. Webb's in the Cornmarket, and beneath it stands Foregate Flowers' kiosk.

(64) GAUMONT CINEMA. Double Disney: *Blackbeard's Ghost* and *Old Yeller*, for the benefit of those trapped in a long summer holiday.

(65) TRAFFIC WARDENS. A perfectly human, harmless species, provided you play fair, but — and it's not easy to say this — doesn't the cap of the right-hand one have a very slight hint of SS about it?

(66) ODEON CINEMA. Hoping to lure the audience to its screen with *The Devil Rides Out*. To the right, J. C. Baker's is rising up from the ashes of the fire which gutted it on 2 June 1966.

(68) MARKET'S OPEN! Early customers at Angel Street.

(71) THE CROSS. Ladders to the left and right of him, the driver folds arms across the wheel and watches his Ombersley Road bus being photographed.

(72) HIGH STREET, 8.50 a.m. Summer Sales and the 'Genuine Reductions' are here. Are these girls hoping to 'snap-up' a bargain or two, or are they sales assistants, waiting to be snapped at?

(74) INTERNATIONAL STORES. The 'notebook' has been spotted by a hurrying couple, causing them to miss the low prices on the window.

(75) HIGH STREET, 8.53 a.m. There are a lot of sales – Bobby's, Ratner's, K's Shoe Shop and Manfield's with the Securicor van parked outside. Apart from J. W. Cassidy & Son Ltd., the jewellers, only Wimbush have opted-out of this seasonal pastime. Come to think of it, a summer sale of bread and cakes might not sound too convincing.

(76) ST SWITHIN'S STREET. His hips seem well enough as he attempts to stride out of the photograph.

(77) SLIGHT CONGESTION in St Swithin's Street. A bread delivery van, a tractor and trailer tailed by a car, and a row of parked vans all contribute to the festivities. Well, some of the pedestrians are happy enough.

(79) THE OLD LAW AND ORDER CHANGETH. Less than a year ago he would have been a member of the City Police Force, but on 1 October 1967 it became West Mercia Police.

(80) THE CROSS, 9 a.m. and the day begins to bustle. Behind the quickly-stepping girls is the same Securicor van that was seen in front of Manfield's, seven minutes ago – page 44. It is now parked in front of the National Provincial Bank.

(81) BOUND FOR COMER GARDENS, a W12 swings round the corner from St Nicholas Street.

(82) WAYSIDE PULPIT on the side wall of St Nicholas Church: 'Unhappy people are those who seek only their own happiness'. If only all sermons could say as much in so few words.

(83) THE CO-OP'S FOR SALE – but only because they're moving to a new building on the other side of St Nicholas Street. Almost hiding behind the parked car is their energetic catering manager, Mr Bollen, preparing for the day's functions. He always seems able to pop-up at the crucial moment, in time to save the lost-for-words bridegroom's floundering speech from drowning.

(84) QUEEN STREET. Gardner's Bakery and – left – a tiny piece of Lowesmoor's Union Inn. (You can park your car there now, but watch for the puddles during the monsoon season.)

(86) CLEAN SWEEP. Proprietor wields broom, potential customer studies window at Walter Dudfield's gentlemen's outfitters in Lowesmoor. (Swept away now, to provide Sansome Walk with a wider mouth.)

(87) BETTY & DEREK BROWN are newsagents in Lowesmoor, next to H. C. Wall & Co., the electrical contractors. They stock just about everything, but it is the day's headlines which first command attention, so please turn the page to find out what some of the papers are saying today, 3 August 1968.

(88) A QUICK RUN DOWN THE RACK: *Daily Express* – 'The Pill. *Express* Poll on the Pope's decision'; *Daily Mirror* – 'ITV Shows Face A Weekend Of . . .' (presumably disruption); *Sporting Chronicle* – 'Beau Darling One to Bank on'; *Sun* – 'Czechs Poised For Victory'; *Daily Mail* – 'Hubbard – Man of millions still dominates Scientology', and '80 live as plane crashes'. (The *Express* appears to have cost 5d. as probably did the *Mail*. Neither of them had yet developed tabloid tendencies.)

(89) PERSONAL SERVICE. Betty Brown hands change to her customer. (Small change in 1988 isn't nearly as small as it was then.)

(90) UNFORESEEN ASSOCIATIONS: pills, tabloids, and now, tablets. The monumental H. K. Brown sculpts around the corner in Silver Street.

(91) SILVER STREET was the birthplace of Worcester Royal Infirmary in 1745. It's a rather charming, higgledy-piggledy sort of street, untouched by time, if not by traffic. (Time later touched it to the ground, for the sake of the traffic.)

(92) UNPROMISING FORECAST. A quick dash over to the weather centre – adjoining the King's School ground – produces a near-unanimous verdict from the experts.

(95) THE FLAT EARTH SOCIETY'S GALA DAY. The King's School groundsman prepares the pitch for the afternoon match.

(96) ROUGH RIDE. Bouncing over the bumps in Comer Gardens.

(98 & 99) FROM ST CLEMENT'S CHURCH TOWER in Henwick Road, these four general views show some old and new faces on the west side of the city. The flats in Tybridge Street are nearing completion and to their left, St Clement's School is backed by waste-ground on either side of Tybridge Street . . . .

(100 & 101) ... Still further left – looking roughly east – the Glover's Needle and the electricity works' funnels break the Newtown and Tolladine skylines. Finally, a view of Henwick Road, curving towards the Bull Ring. The Grosvenor Arms is in the right foreground, whilst the distant left is occupied by the old Worcester Windshields factory – formerly the tramway depot.

(102) PERMANENT WAYSIDE COTTAGE, close to the railway at Henwick Road. It looks as if it is ripe for removal.

(103 & 108) HENWICK ROAD LEVEL CROSSING, from St Clement's tower and then from the trackside. (It is continental now, not as reassuring to cross and boring to look at.)

(114) THREE VIEWS FROM BLOCKHOUSE BRIDGE. This one is typical of the 'backstage' scenery in any city.

(117) HELLO, SUNSHINE! The brief appearance referred to in the introduction. It shines on Worcester Engineering Company's factory at the corner of Carden Street and Foundry Street. (Hardy & Padmore – right – had closed in 1967.)

(119) CANAL CRUISING. Emerging from Blockhouse lock and heading for Sidbury, Diglis and the Severn.

(121) WOODBINE WILLIE'S CHURCH — St Paul's, from the desolate other side of the road. The area is about to be redeveloped.

(124) MIDLAND ROAD, seen from Lea & Perrins' factory, looking towards the distant Hollymount and Tolladine. (Today, the fuel has disappeared, and the middle-ground area has become a free car-park.)

(130) CRATES AND CRATES AND CRATES – of Lea & Perrins products – not necessarily sauce – ready for shipment to all parts of the world. The courtyard clock reads 11.40 a.m.

(131) THE BROWNING VISION. 35a, Wyld's Lane, where they have an ever-changing selection of second-hand furniture and bits and pieces. The oval mirror looks a bargain at only £2.5s. 0d.

(132) LONDON ROAD, at its lower end – it actually finishes at the pedestrian crossing and the Loch Ryan Hotel is unexpectedly found to be in Sidbury.

(133) LONDON ROAD HILL. Any competent dentist would tell it to have the gaps filled. Lower left is a car-park cavity for the restaurant shown in the previous view. Half-way up the hill are posters for Haig's whisky, Colmore Depot, Harp lager and Cadbury's chocolate – more CDMs. The old tram standards are still in use as street lighting. The lull in traffic is not simply unusual for midday on a summer Saturday, it must constitute some kind of a record.

(135) SIDBURY, FROM WYLD'S LANE CORNER. All traffic coming from London Road has to turn into Bath Road and Commandery Road. Approaching us is a rare vision; a motor-cycle combination whose rider carries an 'L' plate and has his wife and child in the side-car. (Happy birthday, if you were the young passenger in UOC 832 – it can't be long before your 21st.)

(136) QUESTION MARK. (This must have been taken from somewhere around the bottom end of Nash's Passage. Today, the girls would be about to cross City Walls Road.)

(138) ST MICHAEL'S WAY? The bridge doesn't prevent the two sides of the Shambles from falling apart, but provides goods access for Marks & Spencer. Function triumphs over beauty.

(139) NO BULLS HERE, PLEASE – there simply isn't room. How the amazing Pratley's manage to pile up so much china in their shop is a mystery. Don't they *ever* break any?

(140) FAMILIAR FACIAS. Chas Smith & Son; James Andrews; George Mason. And familiar faces filling the street.

(141) MARKET MODERNISED. The Market Hall's Shambles face, after lifting. (More recently it has undergone major internal surgery.)

(143) SATISFIED CUSTOMERS leaving Dorothy Parker's shop in City Arcade. The business was previously next to the Swan Inn, Pump Street, before demolition made way for the new church.

(146 & 147/8) LUNCHTIME PARADE. High Street at its busiest in these three views. The time is 12.20 p.m. and few words are needed, though it is, perhaps, indicative of declining motoring manners when a 'special' policeman has to shepherd pedestrians at their own crossing.

(149) LOTUS BLOSSOMS IN BULL ENTRY, as shoppers quietly charge up the steps, *en route* for the High Street arena.

(150) ENDANGERED SPECIES? Is the West Mercian Panda's survival threatened, and will it become as rare a sight as policemen on the street?

(152) ALL HALLOWS, from the steps of All Saints Church. The Dines Green bus is passing with a loaded lower deck, but few passengers upstairs to enjoy the views.

(153) GLASS ACRES. Skylights filter the view of the Severn, liberally sprinkled with anglers on its west bank. Gascoyne's warehouse is on the left.

(154) ALL HALLOWS AGAIN. Cars from Deansway are waiting to turn into Broad Street. The traffic-lights are either not working or have not come into operation yet.

(156) ALL SAINTS CHURCH. Looking up at it from its new, namesake road. The time is now 12.35 p.m.

(157) NEWPORT STREET. Outside an unnamed fruit & vegetable shop. Jaffas are 5 for 1s., Melons 2s. 6d., Runner beans 1s. per lb. and Cauliflowers 1s. & 1s. 6d.

(159) BUS STATION. A 315 Stourbridge via Kidderminster has a few passengers, eager to depart, but the driver has nipped off in search of tea, or something.

(160) NORTH QUAY. A mini-forest of lampposts, flagpoles, signs and railings.

(161) THE S.S. *BELLE* leaves from here with hour-long trips to Camp Lock. Adults 5s., Children 2s.

(164) CROFT ROAD. At the back of the car-park, a new road is being laid to the Grandstand on Pitchcroft.

(165) RAISED EYEBROWS? Ladies to the right, Gents to the left, beneath the Croft Road railway arches.

(167) NORTH QUAY. A Midland Red 144 starts the Birmingham journey from Newport Street. Would someone please tell the driver he is in the wrong lane?

(170) THE BUTTS. Here's an old-fashioned sort of establishment. It may say Clackson Upholsterer, but the shop seems also to cater for human upholstery, with its cream cakes and ice-cream.

(171) GARDEN SHOP. Not easy to see who owns it. Dixon's used to, a year or two ago; now, Holtham's name has appeared in the window.

(172) INFIRMARY WALK. A small child disappears through the door of the old Auntie's Snack Bar. A hint of the Paul Pry is on the left.

(173) THE CORN EXCHANGE. Lunchtime 'busyness' at the bottom of Angel Street.

(175) MOTORWAY EXPRESS. The M5 Motorway has been open for about four years, enabling coaches to provide a faster Birmingham service than the 144 can offer.

(176) MEALCHEAPEN STREET, at its junction with the Shambles. Posters for Swan Vestas and 'Elastic Money' relieve the whiteness of the wall above Foss Pet & Poultry Foods.

(177) THE SHAMBLES, from the north end, and even busier than before. Samuel's clock puts the time at 12.55 p.m.

(178) LITTLE BOOT'S — as it is often referred to — on the corner of Trinity and Mealcheapen Street.

(179) F. DURRANT & SON. Established 1812 for the sale of guns, ammunition, fishing tackle and sports goods.

(180) THE CORNMARKET. An Everton's coach and R. A. Phillips' van block the view of W & F. Webb Ltd.

(181) HOLTHAM & CO. LTD. Established 1801 and still prettily occupying the New Street corner of the Cornmarket.

(182) 'WHAT CAN YOU ALLOW ME ON THIS?' Thompson's Pledge Office – pawnbrokers, in other words – is in New Street, next to the tongue-twisting Nash's Passage – (and try saying that a few times, whether or not your breath has reached crystal-turning density.)

(183) THE EVER POPULAR, THE ONE AND ONLY – Fish & Chips. The lunchtime queue at Laslett Street has overflowed the shop and run out of the picture.

(185) ST JOHN'S. Having attained its ultimate height, one of the Tybridge Street blocks of flats flatly blocks the view from the Bull Ring. A few yards ahead of the two girls is the entrance to the old tramway depot.

(186) HENWICK ROAD. Street furniture outside St John's Post Office.

(188) THE CITY SHOW, AT PITCHCROFT. Among the attractions are vintage and veteran vehicles like this Thornycroft.

(190) WORCESTER PAST. The City Library's photographic display arouses keen interest.

(191) IMPERIAL TRANSPORT. A penny-farthing earns intensely pensive admiration.

(193) A ROUNDABOUT isn't doing very good business. Maybe they'll make it up on the swings — if there are any.

(196) AROUND THE BOATS, a critically approving audience studies radio-controlled models on an artificial pool.

(201) HYDRAGENTLEMAN. The real head is in there, somewhere, as he peddles his balloons.

(202) 'WE BACK BRITAIN', says Yorky's van, and the customers respond by backing Yorky. An ice-cream sundae is 1s. 6d.

(206) UNIFORM DIVERSITY. Outside, in Severn Terrace, officials keep an eye on whatever needs to have eyes kept upon it.

(207 & 208) FOREGATE STREET. The Public Library is having a quiet afternoon.

(209) BROMWICH ROAD. Cars queue for the city centre. The good news is that Fina will sell you a 12-volt battery for £3 19s. 6d. The notice bearing this cheery message stands before a battery of flats.

(210) SATISFACTORY START. The Old Vigornians are batting on the King's School ground and have reached 21 for 0. Next man in is a relaxed and confident T. E. A. Mackie.

(212) EFFECTIVE ELEGANCE. Mesmerised fielders remain motionless whilst the ball speeds away – perhaps you can spot it.

(213) SLOWER PROGRESS. Outside, in New Road, drivers aren't scoring anything like as quickly.

(214) WHO CARES ABOUT PROGRESS? Anglers have all the time a day offers, in order to achieve peace of mind — if little else, sometimes.

(215) BRIDGES ARE FOR BEING NEAR, not for rushing across to get to the other side.

(216) NOVEL CAMP SITE. Don't often see this sort of thing on the south-west bank. Could be a visitor from up north, in which case, full marks for t'enterprise.

(218) NO MARKS FOR THIS ONE. Was it really necessary to dedicate this prime space to the patron saint of parking fees?

(219) CARS EVERYWHERE. Let's get away from the traffic ...

(220) ... AND FIND SOME PEACE IN THE PARK. At Cripplegate, the customary floral display publicises the show already visited — it is its 21st anniversary.

(221) ROSES ALL THE WAY ...

(222) ... UNTIL THE RETURN TO REALITY.

(226) WOODS ON THE GREEN. Bowls at Cripplegate Park.

(230) THE BULL RING. At the junction with Henwick Road. St John's Post Office is operated by R. S. Skan.

(234) CURE FOR SHORT CIRCUITS? Smith & Sons are on the opposite side of the Bull Ring (they closed-down in 1987), next to G. A. Lewis the butcher.

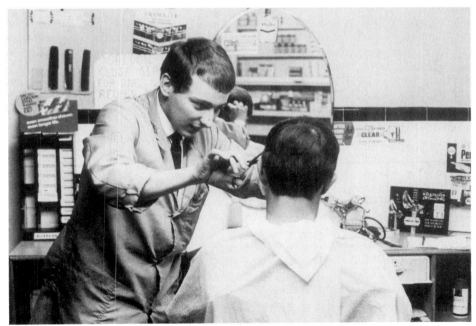

(235) CARE OVER SHORT HAIRCUT. Terry Bourne administers a tidy trim.

(236) STRIPED FACILITY. Dutifully drawn-up at the pedestrian crossing in St John's is a car from the Fagence School of Motoring. (Today, traffic-lights control this junction.)

THE SON OF T. M HOPKINS,
OF THIS CITY, HOP MERCHANT.
JOHN GARMSTON, BORN 1858, DIED 1871.
JONATHAN EDWARD, BORN 1868, DIED 1870.

(237) UNUSUAL HEADSTONE. Watched over by angels, John Garmston Hopkins rests in peace at St John's churchyard – or, at least a photograph of his 13 year-old corpse does, preserved behind glass for all to see. He died in 1871.

(238) WEDDING DAY. Guests arriving at St John's. Many a bridegroom has first fortified himself at the Bell, opposite, before attacking the path to the church.

(239) THE ONLOOKER. From a safe distance, the proprietor of St John's Cycle Shop observes the proceedings.

(241) REDUNDANT CINEMA. St John's has been standing empty and idle for a long time, awaiting a buyer. It may have been known to some as 'The Flea-pit', but it was a lot of fun. From the back row of the circle you almost needed binoculars to see the screen.

(242) WASTELAND seeks a builder; the church awaits the bride.

(244) CONGESTED STREET. The Rushwick bus threading its way between parked cars in St John's.

(245) F. NORMAN & SONS LTD. St John's Garage, with a shirt-sleeved John Norman heading for the pumps. Mobil Super Special is 6s. a gallon, and the lesser grades from 5s. $4\frac{1}{2}$ d. – 5s. 8d.

(247) AFTERNOON PERAMBULATION. The baby's mother has popped into the pharmacy, leaving it outside to count the cars.

(249) ODD ARCHITECTURAL ASSORTMENT. The Bush, at the top of Tybridge Street, the 'Norman-arched' Gents in New Road and the flats, yet again.

(251) HOUSING FASHIONS. The shape of things arrived. Houses in Mallard Close. Around the corner, a similar one is for sale at £4,695.

(257) OPEN WIDE. Filling-time at Hylton Road. Esso Extra is shunned – 6s. a gallon – for a more modest grade. Through the trees, a glimpse of the Grandstand Hotel, across river.

(259) HYLTON ROAD. Redevelopment of warehouse and factory premises.

(260) BEYOND REDEMPTION. A small sign reads: Severn Garage, 12 Hylton Road. But where are the pumps and the forecourt?

(261) A LAST LOOK AT THE MARKET, where trade is still brisk, at a time when shops are closing for the day.

(262) BREWERY TOWER. The dominating feature of Lewis Clarke's Ltd. fails to impress the neighbouring Vaults which favours Marston's.

(263) FOR POSTERS. A typical display of what's up, what's on and what's for sale, adorning the Corn Exchange.

(264) THE FOREGATE. Anderson & Virgo, Family & Dispensing Chemists. (Today, it is 'Good News'.)

(265) ANOTHER PRETTY FOREGATE FACE — W. H. Smith's. At one time, newspaper and magazine sales were separated from the main body of the shop by a screen and inner door.

(266) TIME TO GO HOME, 5.45 p.m. and cars are nose to tail from The Cross to The Foregate. Scooterist and passenger are trying to escape from Sansome Street, but seem resigned rather than hopeful.

(268) TEA-TIME EDITION. The man with the umbrella has two piles of Worcester Evening News to dispense before he can call it a day.

(269) HE HAS CUSTOMERS, as overhead the crested bridge supports a departing train aiming for Malvern and Hereford.

(270) OH, WELL DONE! Skilful double-parking is making life difficult for the van pulling out in Angel Street. The Colmore Depot occupies the old Theatre Royal Site.

(271) BLACKFRIARS SQUARE. The development is growing, though still in need of more flesh on the skeleton.

(272) THE TYTHING. The Green Man is flanked by the pharmacy of W. H. Taylor Ltd. and S. G. Gardner's shop.

(273) THE TYTHING. The same side, slightly further on and looking towards Upper Tything and Barbourne.

(275) GHELUVELT PARK. The main gate of the park, whose name commemorates the stand of the Worcestershire Regiment in World War 1.

(276) SPARSELY POPULATED. In this early evening scene, Gheluvelt Park has more poplars than people.

(278) BECALMED BANDSTAND. Surrounded by water, perhaps the ideal place for testing discs for the desert island.

(279) CITY'S QUAINTEST SHOP? Under the name of M. A. Digger, it faces Gheluvelt Park. Today's bargains are cabbage 6*d*. and English new potatoes at 3*d*. per lb.

(280) ARCHITECTURAL LAYER CAKE. Take one low wall with railing, one length of playground, one temporary classroom and one church topped with tower. Set St Stephen's timer at 6.17 p.m. (Wait 20 years or less and all but the final ingredient will have vanished.)

(281) OMBERSLEY ROAD POST OFFICE. Under L & M. Simpson who haven't yet closed their door. The hours are long in this business, especially when combined with being a newsagent.

(282) OMBERSLEY ROAD ANACHRONISM. Not many clues to 1968 in evidence as a couple of vintage models head for home after the City Show.

(283) EYES DOWN FOR A BLANK SCREEN. The Northwick Cinema has changed allegiance and now housey houses the Vogue Bingo & Social Club. Members are seen arriving for a 7 p.m. start.

(285) SHOPS TO LET. Next to the Northwick, these newly-built units await their first tenants.

(289) A FACE LIKE THE BACK OF A JAVELIN. Today's mystery object, viewed from Droitwich Road.

(290) IT IS A JAVELIN! Standing at the entrance to Worcester ATC Headquarters at Perdiswell. (Was thrown in 1987.)

(291) PEACE AT PERDISWELL LOCK, from Bilford Road bridge.

(292 & 293) CANAL AND LOCK. Two further views at Perdiswell.

(294) ASTWOOD FARM in Bilford Road. (Housing now occupies the land.)

(301) TOLLADINE ROAD, at its junction with Hollymount Road and Teme & Avon Roads.

(303) ROSE AVENUE. A cluster of children round the back of a van.

(306) STATION WALK, from Tolladine Road. The 'no cycling' sign ought to dissuade anyone from pedalling up the steps. It would be a very bumpy ride ...

(307) ... AND STEEP, TOO. Station Walk from the top of the steps.

(308) TRIBUTE TO BATMAN, though he looks vicious enough to eat Robin. Never mind, the artists are sufficiently satisfied to have signed it — Tom and Frank.

(311) SHRUB HILL STATION. Luggage-laden passengers struggling to do what a porter used to do for them.

(313) ANYONE FOR LEAPFROG? It's really rather reasonable – driver, with any size car and up to three passengers can be whisked from Bristol to Totnes for £6 single, £10 return.

(315) RAILWAY OVER RAILINGS. The entrance to Newtown Road from Midland Road.

(316) A TUNNEL OF BRIDGES. Distant cars wait at the far traffic-lights as the near ones are changing to green.

(317) BENEATH THE BRIDGE, looking out from Newtown Road at some of the buildings of Shrub Hill Hospital and Hillborough.

(318) SHEEP SAFELY GRAZING. It's getting late and conditions are slightly hazy, half-way up Newtown Road hill.

(321) THE GOOD OLD CORNER SHOP. This is more of a tri-corner shop, at the junction of Wyld's Lane, London Road and Lark Hill Road.

(322) THEY DON'T BUILD 'EM LIKE THIS ANY MORE. A row of tidy frontages in Sebright Avenue.

(323) EXPANDING BUSINESS. At Navigation Road, T. J. Tresnan & Sons are building a new factory for Worcester Engineering Co. Ltd.

(326) SAFELY MOORED. Boats at Diglis Basin.

(327) CLOISTERED CRAFT AT DIGLIS. (The old Townsend's Flour Mill is now part of 'Royal Worcester'.)

(328) INDEFATIGABLE FISHERS. With river mist rising at Diglis, where the canal joins the Severn, anglers still bait hooks with hope in their hearts.

(329) THE FOUNTAIN INN, Severn Street. The entrance to Worcester Royal Porcelain is across the street.

(330) GIFFARD HOTEL. As yet, Hartley Carpets is the only shop to have opened on this side of the development.

(331) LICHGATE PRECINCT, from its High Street approach. Hartley Carpets is on the extreme right, with Russell & Dorrell barely creeping in on the left. Straight ahead, Sainsbury's have opened, behind the protective, latter-day portcullis. Every other unit is still boarded-up.

(332) HIGH STREET, 8.34 p.m. In the left foreground, a new building stands at the corner of Copenhagen Street, where H. C. Slade Ltd. formerly sold their shoes. Almost directly opposite is the long-established chemist, C. A. Steward, possibly feeling a draught from the adjacent gap left by the Market Hall's demolition.

(335) LIGHTING-UP TIME. The lamps are beginning to come on as a car turns onto the bridge from Hylton Road, and a well-illuminated bus heads for St John's.

(336) AND STILL THEY'RE FISHING. Do they bait their hooks with glow-worms?

(337) UNLIT LAMPS. The post supporting them carries an RAC pointer to the now extinct 21st City of Worcester Show.

(338) NORTH PARADE & NORTH QUAY. The Severn View Hotel stands in front of Midland Shires Farmers Ltd., brokenly reflected in the evening Severn.